The Children's Picture Gallery

30 FAVORITE COLOR ILLUSTRATIONS TO CLIP AND FRAME

Edited by Pasquale Cool

BOUNTY BOOKS
New York

How To Enjoy This Book

When you remove a page from the book, simply cut it out following the dotted lines on the back of each print. Some have one set of dotted lines and will fit into a standard 8″ x 10″ frame. Others have two sets of dotted lines and will fit either a 5″ x 7″ frame or an 8″ x 10″ frame.

To J.L.S.

House Editor: PATRICIA G. HORAN
Book and Cover Design: KEN SANSONE
Production: MURRAY SCHWARTZ

h g f e d c b a

Manufactured in the United States of America.

LIBRARY OF CONGRESS CATALOGING IN PUBLICATION DATA

Main entry under title: The Children's picture gallery.

SUMMARY: Representative works of some early great children's book illustrators: Robinson, Potter, Rackham, Greenaway, Denslow, Brooke, Crane, and Caldecott.
1. Children's literature—Illustrations—Juvenile literature.
[1. Children's literature—Illustrations]
I. Cool, Pasquale, 1947–
NC 965.C45   741.64′2   76-2464
ISBN 0-517-52593-3

The Contents

BEATRIX POTTER

Beatrix Potter (1866-1943) was born and lived in England. She is the author and illustrator of *The Tale of Peter Rabbit, The Tale of Benjamin Bunny* and others. These are among the greatest children's books of all time.

W.W. DENSLOW

William Wallace Denslow (1856-1915) was born in Philadelphia. He was also an author but was most widely known for his illustrations of the original *The Wizard of Oz*.

CHARLES ROBINSON

Charles Robinson (1870-1937) was an English illustrator and lithographer. *Aesop's Fables* was the first of many books he designed and illustrated in his very distinct and descriptive style.

ARTHUR RACKHAM

Arthur Rackham (1867-1939) was a British artist who was known as "The Dean of Fairyland" for his delicate style and imagination. The style he set in *Peter Pan in Kensington Gardens* has not been equalled.

ARTHUR RACKHAM
(continued)

KATE GREENAWAY

Kate Greenaway (1846-1901) invented her own costumes for the children on her pages. She illustrated almost every Mother Goose nursery character and is noted for her brilliant colors and graceful figures.

L. LESLIE BROOKE

Leonard Leslie Brooke spent equal amounts of his eighty years in the nineteenth and twentieth centuries. He is well known for his illustrations of best-loved nursery rhymes.

WALTER CRANE

Walter Crane (1845-1915) illustrated Grimm's and other fairy tales. He studied Japanese color prints, fifteenth century Florentine painting and designed Art Nouveau textiles and wall papers. All of these served to enrich his work.

RANDOLPH CALDECOTT

Randolph Caldecott (1846-1886) was an English artist famous for his jolly pictures of outdoor life, his satirical drawings and his illustrations for children's books. The famed Caldecott medal is named after him.

Ring-a-ring-a-roses,
A pocket full of posies;
Hush! hush! hush! hush!
We're all tumbled down.

Little Bo-Peep has lost her sheep,
And can't tell where to find them;
Leave them alone, and they'll come home,
And bring their tails behind them.

Jack and Jill
Went up the hill,
To fetch a pail of water;
Jack fell down
And broke his crown,
And Jill came tumbling after.

Here am I, little jumping Joan,
When nobody's with me,
I'm always alone.

Georgie Peorgie, pudding and pie,
Kissed the girls and made them cry;
When the girls begin to play,
Georgie Peorgie runs away.